Organize YOUR WRITING

LEVEL H

Lida F. Lim
Margaret C. Moran

New Readers Press

Organize Your Writing Level H
ISBN 978-1-56420-714-2

Copyright © 2007 New Readers Press
New Readers Press
Division of ProLiteracy Worldwide
1320 Jamesville Avenue, Syracuse, New York 13210
www.newreaderspress.com

All rights reserved. No part of this book may be reproduced or transmitted in any form or by any means, electronic or mechanical, including photocopying, recording, or by any information storage and retrieval system, without permission in writing from the publisher.

Printed in the United States of America
9   8   7   6   5   4   3   2   1

All proceeds from the sale of New Readers Press materials support literacy programs in the United States and worldwide.

Contributing Writers: Lauren Hauptman, Judy A. Johnson, Jay S. Winston
Editorial Development: Toppy Editorial
Design and Production Manager: Andrea Woodbury
Illustrations: James Wallace, John Prejza, Jr.
Production Specialists: Jeffrey Smith, Maryellen Casey
Cover Design: James Wallace

Introduction: Before You Begin
   About *Organize Your Writing* 5
   About the Writing Process 6
   Evaluating Your Writing 7

Write to Inform

CHAPTER 1
Narration: Retelling a Personal Experience 8
    Organizing Pattern: Chronological Order

   Lesson 1: Prewriting: Brainstorm, Identify, Organize 10
       Organizing Tools: Listing, Chart, Time Line

   Lesson 2: Writing Your First Draft 14
       Fluency Tip: Transitions That Show Time Order 15

   Lesson 3: Revising Your Draft 17

   Lesson 4: Writing Your Final Draft 18

CHAPTER 2
Exposition: Summarizing a Reading Selection 19
    Organizing Pattern: Order of Importance

   Lesson 1: Prewriting: Identify, Organize 21
       Organizing Tools: Listing, Charts

   Lesson 2: Writing Your First Draft 26
       Fluency Tip: Transitions That Add Information 27

   Lesson 3: Revising Your Draft 28

   Lesson 4: Writing Your Final Draft 30

Write to Describe

CHAPTER 3
Description: Describing a Place 31
    Organizing Pattern: Spatial Order

   Lesson 1: Prewriting: Brainstorm, Select, Organize 33
       Organizing Tools: Listing, Charts, Mapping

   Lesson 2: Writing Your First Draft 37
       Fluency Tip: Words That Show Place 38

   Lesson 3: Revising Your Draft 39

   Lesson 4: Writing Your Final Draft 40

CHAPTER 4
Description: Describing a Person 41
    Organizing Patterns: Order of Importance, Chronological Order

   Lesson 1: Prewriting: Identify, Select, Organize 43
       Organizing Tools: Listing, Chart, Mapping

   Lesson 2: Writing Your First Draft 47
       Fluency Tip: Transitions That Add Information and That Show Time Order 48

   Lesson 3: Revising Your Draft 50

   Lesson 4: Writing Your Final Draft 52

Write to Explain

CHAPTER 5
Exposition: Comparing and Contrasting 53
 Organizing Patterns: Block Arrangement, Order of Importance
- Lesson 1: Prewriting: Identify, Select, Organize 55
 Organizing Tools: Listing, Venn Diagram, Chart
- Lesson 2: Writing Your First Draft 58
 Fluency Tip: Transitions That Show Comparison and Contrast 59
- Lesson 3: Revising Your Draft 60
- Lesson 4: Writing Your Final Draft 62

CHAPTER 6
Exposition: Explaining Cause and Effect 63
 Organizing Pattern: Chronological Order
- Lesson 1: Prewriting: Identify, Brainstorm, Organize 65
 Organizing Tools: Listing, Chart
- Lesson 2: Writing Your First Draft 68
 Fluency Tip: Transitions That Show Cause and Effect 69
- Lesson 3: Revising Your Draft 71
- Lesson 4: Writing Your Final Draft 73

Write to Persuade

CHAPTER 7
Persuasion: Identifying a Problem and Offering a Solution 74
 Organizing Pattern: Problem-to-Solution Order
- Lesson 1: Prewriting: Identify, Brainstorm, Organize 76
 Organizing Tools: Listing, Chart
- Lesson 2: Writing Your First Draft 80
 Fluency Tip: Problem-Solution Signal Words and Phrases 81
- Lesson 3: Revising Your Draft 82
- Lesson 4: Writing Your Final Draft 84

CHAPTER 8
Persuasion: Writing a Letter to Persuade 85
 Organizing Pattern: Logical Order
- Lesson 1: Prewriting: Identify, Brainstorm, Organize 87
 Organizing Tools: Listing, Chart
- Lesson 2: Writing Your First Draft 90
 Fluency Tip: Signal Words and Phrases That Emphasize a Point 92
- Lesson 3: Revising Your Draft 93
- Lesson 4: Writing Your Final Draft 95

Appendix: Transitions and Signal Words and Phrases 96

INTRODUCTION
BEFORE YOU BEGIN

"Good writing is good thinking."

Keep reminding yourself of this sentence as you work through *Organize Your Writing*. To write a clear, understandable paragraph, essay, or report, you need to think clearly about what you are going to say. You cannot just read an assignment and begin writing. You need to think about and plan your writing. Organization is the key to good thinking and good writing. *Organize Your Writing* will help you learn to spend time thinking about and organizing your ideas early in the writing process.

About *Organize Your Writing*

When we talk to people, we present our ideas so they make sense to our listeners. This should also be true for our writing. We need to present our ideas so that they are easy to follow and make sense to our readers. This pattern of presentation is called organization. If the organization does not present information in a way that the reader can follow, the reader will quickly lose interest. Try to make sense out of the following paragraph:

> They argued about what to see, but finally settled on *Return of the Werewolves*. The four friends decided to go to the movies. There were a lot of people in the theater lobby. Each bought a soda and popcorn. They could not find four seats together, so they split up. The friends had to weave their way through to the refreshment stand.

Can you figure out what the four friends did? There is no organization to the paragraph. What happened first? What happened second?

In *Organize Your Writing*, you will learn about and use various patterns of organization. The pattern in each chapter depends on the assignment. Listed below are the organizational patterns used in this book:
- chronological order
- spatial order
- order of importance
- block arrangement
- problem-to-solution order
- logical order

To help you organize your writing, you will be learning to use tools such as brainstorming, identifying, selecting, and combining information. You will also be learning to use graphic organizers. Graphic organizers help you identify what is important and why. They come in a variety of shapes and forms. These patterns of organization and tools can prepare you to write your first draft.

About the Writing Process

As any athlete will tell you, you need to practice if you want to improve your skills. Like athletes, writers need opportunities to practice. In *Organize Your Writing*, you will have many opportunities to practice the writing process. The writing process is a series of steps that ends in an essay, a paragraph, a letter, an editorial, or some other type of writing. In order to become a competent and confident writer, use this process every time you write.

1. Prewrite
- Know what the assignment is and how it will be evaluated.
  Ask yourself: What exactly am I to do? How will this assignment be graded? What must I do to get the highest score possible?

- Brainstorm all the ideas you can think of for the assignment.
  Make a list of all the ideas that come to mind. The more ideas you have, the more choices you will have when you start to organize your writing.

- Select or identify the ideas you want to use.
  Be thoughtful in your choices. Who will read what you write? Thinking about your audience and the purpose of the assignment will help you select which ideas to use.

- Determine the organizing pattern to use.
  You need to choose the pattern that makes the most sense for what you are writing about. It should present your ideas so they are easy for your readers to follow.

2. Write
- Write your first draft.
  Do not stop to worry about a word or a sentence. Do follow your organizing pattern.

3. Revise
- Revise and edit your first draft.
  This is the most important step in the writing process. This is where you will perfect your writing. You will look at the words you have selected, the sentences you have written, and the development of your ideas. You will also look at the mechanics of your writing (spelling, punctuation, and grammar). Ask yourself: Is my writing clear? Is it easy to follow? Could it use some more details? Use the rubric for the assignment as your guide.

4. Write
- Write your final draft.
  You want to be proud of this piece of writing. Make sure that it reflects the competent and confident writer that you are.

As you carefully work through this book, keep in mind: Practice makes good writing permanent.

Evaluating Your Writing

In each chapter, you are asked to review this rubric before you write your final draft. If you know what is expected, chances are you will do better on the assignment.

GENERAL WRITING RUBRIC

	4 points	3 points	2 points	1 point	0 points
Assignment Requirements and Focus	• Fulfills all parts of the assignment • Stays focused on the topic of the assignment	• Fulfills most parts of the assignment • Stays mostly focused on the topic but wanders off the topic once or twice	• Meets some parts of the assignment • Does not stay focused on the topic	• Meets only part of the assignment • Does not stay focused on the topic	• Writing is off the topic
Organization	• Has a beginning, a middle, and an end • Follows the organizing pattern described in the chapter	• Has a beginning, a middle, and an end • Follows the organizing pattern taught in the chapter, but ideas wander a little, or unnecessary details are included	• Begins and ends abruptly • Does not follow any pattern of organization and contains unnecessary details	• Presents no introduction or conclusion • Does not show any organization	
Development	• Provides a main idea and specific details	• Provides a main idea, but only has a few brief details	• Provides a weak description of the main idea and has few details	• Does not present a main idea or supporting details	
Fluency	• Uses transitions and signal words and phrases to make the writing flow smoothly	• Uses some transitions and signal words and phrases to make the writing flow smoothly	• Uses only one or two transitions or signal words and phrases	• Does not use transitions or signal words and phrases	

Before You Begin 7

INFORMING

CHAPTER 1

Organizing Pattern:
Chronological Order

Narration
Retelling a Personal Experience

A story about something that happened is a **narrative**. For example, a sports report of a football game is a narrative. A person can tell a **personal narrative** about something that happened to him or her. When you tell a friend what you did on the weekend, you are telling a personal narrative.

A story is made up of a series of events, or incidents. One incident follows another until you have the whole story. Whether you tell a personal story or write one, you have to make the order of events very clear. The best way to organize a narrative is by using chronological order.

Chronological order is the order in which events occur. To tell a story clearly, you need to begin with the first incident. Then you tell the incidents in the order in which they occurred until you reach the last one. Chronological order helps the reader follow what is happening in the story.

When a person tells a personal narrative, his or her voice, facial expressions, and body language add interest to the story. In writing a personal narrative, you have only words. You need to select your words carefully to create a picture of what is happening for your readers. Vivid words—specific nouns and descriptive adjectives and adverbs—will add interest to your writing. Which of the following sentences tells you more?

- A boy rode his bike down the road.
- A red-haired boy on a mountain bike performed wheelies down the dusty road.

In this chapter, you will be using listing, a chart, and a time line to help you organize your personal narrative.

Try It!

Read the selection "Learning to Play Basketball." Think about a time when you learned to do something new. Some possibilities are inline skating, using a digital camera, knitting, cooking a new dish, playing a musical instrument or new sport, and building or fixing something. Select a skill and write a personal narrative explaining what happened when you learned this new skill. Use vivid words so your story comes alive.

Read It!

Learning to Play Basketball

The year I turned 12, I went from very short to very tall in just one summer. In my first PE class, the new coach asked if I played basketball. When I said I was too short, he laughed. I asked what was so funny. Then it hit me. I was looking down at the other guys in the class when I used to look up. I was now the tallest kid in the class! I was big enough to play basketball—my dream.

On the way home that first day of school, I saw some guys playing a pick-up game in the park. I walked over, and one of them said I could be on his team. Being tall did not seem to matter much. The kids moved so fast that I hardly ever got the ball. When I did, I would shoot, but the ball would not even come close to the basket. I started to walk away, but Ernie stopped me. Ernie was a couple of years ahead of me in school. He wanted to know why I was leaving. I said it was because I was such a terrible player. Ernie said that no one is good right from the start! Then he gave me some advice. He told me that I should never quit what I start. He asked me to come back and play some more. I did, and I played with them for the rest of the afternoon. I was still pretty bad, but I did not quit. Before I left, Ernie gave me some more advice. He told me that I needed to get a ball and practice.

The next day after school, I borrowed a basketball from my older brother. I went out back and shot baskets in the hoop attached to the garage. For the first hour or two, I missed every shot. Then I started getting it closer to the basket. After a while, I started making some baskets. I did that every day after school for the rest of the week. By the weekend, I was making most of my shots. On Saturday and Sunday, I practiced some more. By then, I decided that I was good enough to try playing with Ernie and the guys again.

After school on Monday, I went to the park. I was going to show them what I could do. They were still too fast for me, and after all that practice I still missed most of my shots. Ernie gave me some more advice. He told me that first I needed to keep working on shooting. Second, I needed to start running every day to work on my speed. Third, I needed to keep playing with the guys to put the two skills together. Last, I needed to learn how to pass to others on my team. Ernie said that teamwork is just as important as having my own skills.

I listened to what he said. I started running and playing with the guys in the park whenever I could. Once I got fast enough to get the ball more often, I learned to pass. I got to be a pretty good player—thanks to Ernie and a lot of hard work.

REREAD THE ASSIGNMENT. THINK ABOUT WHAT YOU ARE TO DO.

INFORMING

LESSON 1
PREWRITING

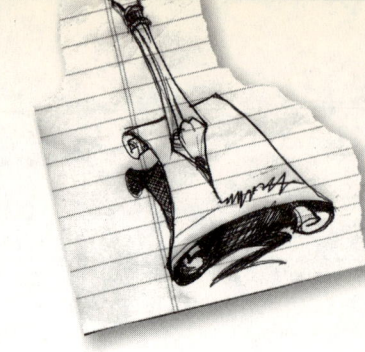

Step 1. Brainstorm

The assignment asks you to write about learning a new skill. What experience of learning a new skill will you choose? To help you decide, first think of a list of skills that were once new to you. Brainstorming will help you.

Brainstorming is making a list of everything that comes to mind about a topic. You do not evaluate your ideas as you write them. You just list as many ideas as you can. You will evaluate them later. Remember: The more ideas you list now, the more ideas you will have to choose from when you plan your essay.

1. Write your list of new skills.

_____   _____

_____   _____

_____   _____

2. The assignment tells you to write about learning only one new skill. You need to narrow your list to your final topic. How do you decide which experience to select? Reread the list you brainstormed and think about answers to the following questions:
   • Which experience do you remember most clearly?
   • Which skill was the hardest or the most fun to learn?
   • Which skill gives you the greatest satisfaction to have learned?
   • Which skill do you use a lot?

   Write the skill that will be the topic of your essay.

   _____

3. Why did you choose that particular skill and learning experience?

   _____

   _____

Step 2. Identify Details

Your details should create a picture in the reader's mind of what happened as you learned your new skill. Do not just tell your reader what happened. Use specific nouns and descriptive adjectives and adverbs that will show your reader what happened.

The most interesting stories have many details. What happened? When? Where? Reread the story "Learning to Play Basketball" on page 9. As you read, notice all the details that the writer uses. He tells you where he played basketball. He names the person who gave him advice. He tells you which days he practiced and where.

The story about your new skill should have as much information for your readers. A What/Who/When/Where/What Happened chart can help you remember information.

1. Complete the following chart. First, complete the column about "Learning to Play Basketball." Use the answers to help you fill in the column for "My Topic."

Question	"Learning to Play Basketball"	My Topic
WHAT?		
WHO?		
WHEN?		
WHERE?		
WHAT HAPPENED?		

Retelling a Personal Experience

INFORMING

2. Reread "Learning to Play Basketball." Notice how the writer uses details to describe each incident that occurred while he was learning to play basketball.

   Write two details from paragraph 4.

   _____

   _____

Make your personal narrative come alive in the same way. To do this, you will need interesting details about each incident. Use the "What Happened" row of your chart on page 11 to help you get started.

3. Write each incident in the first row below. If you have more than three incidents, use a separate sheet of paper.

4. Brainstorm as many details about each incident as you can remember. Write the details below each incident.

1. _____   2. _____   3. _____

Chapter 1: Narration

Step 3. Organize Your Ideas

To organize your writing you need to put the answers to "What Happened?" in chronological order, the order in which the events occurred. Like the writer of "Learning to Play Basketball," you probably learned your skill over a period of time. You will need to put the different things you did in the order in which they occurred. Time lines are useful tools in helping you organize events in chronological order.

1. **Use the time line below to put the incidents you listed on page 12 in chronological order. Write each one on a new line. If you want to write about more than three incidents, use a separate piece of paper.**

   1. _____

   2. _____

   3. _____

2. **Add to column 2 the details you will use from the list you brainstormed on page 12. Write the details for each incident in the order in which you will use them.**

3. **Review the details that you wrote. Add specific nouns and descriptive adjectives and adverbs to create a picture for your reader.**

Retelling a Personal Experience

INFORMING

LESSON 2
WRITING YOUR FIRST DRAFT

Before you begin to write, review the rubric on page 7. You will evaluate your essay against it.

Guide

Introduction

PARAGRAPH 1
- Includes the topic sentence that states the skill you learned

Body

PARAGRAPH 2
- Describes the first incident in detail

PARAGRAPH 3
- Describes the second incident in detail

PARAGRAPH 4
- Describes the third incident in detail

Conclusion

PARAGRAPH 5
- Restates the skill you learned
- States how you feel about learning the skill

Fluency Tip

Transitions That Show Time Order

To help make your narrative read smoothly, use transitions that show time. **Transitions** are bridges. They connect one idea to the next. Use some of the following words and phrases to move from one event to the next in your personal narrative:

a few days ago

a week ago

after

after a while

at last

before

finally

first, second, third, . . .

immediately

later

next

right away

soon, sooner

then, by then

INFORMING

Retelling a Personal Experience

LESSON 3
REVISING YOUR DRAFT

Revising means improving. As you revise your essay, focus on chronological order and the details that describe each incident. Did you write about the incidents in the order they happened? Did you make your narrative interesting by using vivid details?

Use the chart below to compare the model essay "Learning to Play Basketball" with your essay. Focus on how the writer developed the time order.

Question	Model Essay	My Essay
1. What three incidents are described?		
2. What is the topic sentence?		
3. How many paragraphs are in the body?		
4. How many details describe the second incident?		
5. What is the writer's conclusion?		
6. What time-order transitions are used in the essay?		

Retelling a Personal Experience

INFORMING

LESSON 4
WRITING YOUR FINAL DRAFT

Before you begin to write your final draft, review what you have learned and practiced in this chapter.

1. **What type of writing did you do in this chapter?**

   _____

2. **What three steps helped you organize your writing by chronological order?**

   _____

3. **What three tools did you use to pull your ideas together?**

   _____

4. **List four time-order transitions that will make your writing flow more smoothly when you use chronological order.**

   _____

5. **What do you like about your essay?**

   _____

   _____

   _____

Before you write your final draft, review the rubric on page 7. You will evaluate your essay against it. Be sure you know what is needed for an excellent essay.

WRITE YOUR FINAL DRAFT ON SEPARATE PAPER, OR USE A COMPUTER.

CHAPTER 2

Organizing Pattern:
Order of Importance

Exposition
Summarizing a Reading Selection

Exposition is writing that explains and informs. A **summary** is a type of exposition because it explains information. A summary
- is a very short version of an original piece of writing
- uses only the most important points and details
- is stated in the summarizer's own words
- does not include the summarizer's opinions
- includes the author and title of the original work.

A summary may be as much as 50 to 60 percent shorter than the original piece of writing. This is because the purpose of a summary is to highlight only the essential points of the original writing.

Summaries generally follow the same pattern.
- A summary begins with a statement of the main idea, or theme, of the original piece.
- The essential, or main, points of the piece are stated next.
- Only the most important detail or details are included for each essential point.
- The conclusion restates the main idea of the original piece.

Summaries follow the organizational pattern of the original piece of writing. The author of the selection on page 20 uses order of importance. You will also use order of importance for your summary of this piece.

You will use listing and charts to help identify and organize the information for your summary.

INFORMING

Try It!

Read the selection "Emergency Medical Technicians." Write a one-paragraph summary of the article.

Read It!

The Work of Emergency Medical Technicians
by Lauren Hauptman

The emergency medical technician (EMT) field is growing. In many places, professional EMT workers are replacing volunteers. EMTs receive formal training and certification. The National Registry of Emergency Medical Technicians (NREMT) lists four levels of emergency service providers: First Responder, EMT-Basic, EMT-Intermediate, and EMT-Paramedic.

First Responder is the first level of EMTs. First Responders must complete an education program developed by the federal Department of Transportation. They may also receive state training and certification. First Responders have to pass one written exam and one practical exam before they can begin working. These emergency workers are usually the first to arrive at the scene of an accident or sudden illness. They handle crises such as bleeding, shock, obstructed airways, and traumatic or violent injuries. First Responders must know cardiopulmonary resuscitation (CPR) and how to help women give birth.

The next level of workers, EMT-Basic, must also pass written and practical examinations. These tests are administered by the state or the NREMT. EMT-Basics combine classroom instruction with spending time in emergency rooms and riding in ambulances. Like First Responders, they learn how to manage trauma, bleeding, and breathing difficulties. They also learn how to handle cardiac emergencies such as heart attacks and cardiac arrest. Like first responders, EMT-Basics can help mothers with emergency childbirth.

EMT-Intermediate workers fall under the third level of expertise. They have already been certified as EMT-Basics. As EMT-Intermediates, they have more complex duties. In addition to knowing all the procedures that EMT-Basics do, they take courses about specific kinds of emergencies. They may focus on shock and trauma, learning how to give fluids intravenously (through the vein). EMT-Intermediates may also concentrate on cardiac care and learn how to recognize different cardiac emergencies.

EMT-Paramedic workers receive the most advanced level of training and certification. After they are certified as EMT-Intermediates, they take additional courses. They learn to administer medicines and operate complex equipment. Some paramedics find the work so rewarding that they go back to school to become physicians or directors of emergency services.

EMTs derive great satisfaction from their jobs. A person who likes to help others might find being an emergency service worker a great career.

REREAD THE ASSIGNMENT. THINK ABOUT WHAT YOU ARE TO DO.

LESSON 1
PREWRITING

Step 1. Identify the Information

The first step in writing your summary is to identify the information you need to include in it. What is the piece about? What are the essential points? Which details are the most important to include?

1. The topic or main idea of a piece is usually found in the introduction. Sometimes the main idea is directly stated, and sometimes you must infer it, or figure it out, from the information in the paragraph. In this article, you must infer the main idea.

   Write the main idea of "The Work of Emergency Medical Technicians."

   _____
   _____

2. Next, you need to identify the essential points of the article. The writer has built paragraphs 2, 3, 4, and 5 around one essential point each.

   Write the essential point for each paragraph in your own words. Label each point by paragraph number.

   _____
   _____
   _____
   _____
   _____
   _____
   _____

Summarizing a Reading Selection

INFORMING

Complete the chart on page 23 by following these steps:

3. List the essential point for each paragraph in column 1.

4. Reread the article, looking for important details about each essential point that you just wrote.

   In column 2, list at least four supporting details for each essential point. Remember to write them in your own words.

5. Review the details you have identified on the chart on page 23. The definition of summary states that only the most important details are used in a summary. How do you decide which are the most important? The most important details are the ones that

   - are the most necessary in explaining each essential point
   - if left out, would make your summary incomplete and even confusing.

   Identify the two supporting details that best explain the essential points of each paragraph. Cross out the supporting details that you are not going to use.

6. The last paragraph of the article is the conclusion. It wraps up the article by presenting a concluding statement.

   Write in your own words the conclusion from the article.

   _____
   _____
   _____
   _____

Chapter 2: Exposition

Essential Point	Supporting Details for Each Essential Point
Paragraph 2	
Paragraph 3	
Paragraph 4	
Paragraph 5	

INFORMING

Summarizing a Reading Selection

Step 2. Organize Essential Points and Details

In writing a summary, you follow the organization of the original piece of writing. The writer of the article about EMTs develops her paragraphs in order of importance. She starts with the first level of EMTs and moves to the fourth and highest level.

Your summary needs to include the essential points and also details to describe and explain the essential points. Because the original writing is in order of importance, your details should also be presented in order of importance.

1. **Reread the chart on page 23. Number the details in order of importance for each essential point. Write 1 or 2 next to each supporting detail that you are going to use for each essential point.**

2. The chart on page 23 may be hard to read with all the crossing out and numbering. Sometimes before you begin writing, it helps to rewrite information to make it clear. This chart will be your clean working copy. The little bit of time it takes to rewrite now can make writing your first draft easier.

   Complete the chart on page 25 to organize your information. You do not have to write complete sentences. Write words or phrases that will help you remember your ideas when you begin to write.

You need to do more than restate the essential points and their most important supporting details. Like all good pieces of writing, your summary needs a topic sentence and a conclusion.

3. **The topic sentence of a summary states the theme of the piece being summarized. It also includes the title of the article and the author. Write your topic sentence.**

   _____

   _____

4. **The conclusion restates the main idea of the piece being summarized. Write your concluding statement.**

   _____

   _____

   _____

Main idea	
• Essential idea #1	
— Supporting detail #1	
— Supporting detail #2	
• Essential idea #2	
— Supporting detail #1	
— Supporting detail #2	
• Essential idea #3	
— Supporting detail #1	
— Supporting detail #2	
• Essential idea #4	
— Supporting detail #1	
— Supporting detail #2	
Concluding idea	

INFORMING

Summarizing a Reading Selection

INFORMING

LESSON 2
WRITING YOUR FIRST DRAFT

Before you begin to write, review the rubric on page 7. You will evaluate your essay against it.

Guide

Topic Sentence
- Is the first sentence of the paragraph
- States the main idea of the piece being summarized
- Identifies the title and author of the piece being summarized

Body of Paragraph
- Presents essential points in the same order as presented in the original
- Presents the most important supporting details for each essential point

Concluding Sentence
- Restates the main idea of the piece being summarized

Chapter 2: Exposition

Fluency Tip

Transitions That Add Information

Transitions make it easier for readers to follow the development of your ideas. Use some of the following transitions as you add information to your summary paragraph:

- additionally
- along with
- also
- another
- as well as
- besides
- finally
- first, second, third, . . .
- for example
- for instance
- however
- in addition
- in fact
- last
- more/most importantly
- next
- too

INFORMING

Summarizing a Reading Selection

INFORMING

LESSON 3
REVISING YOUR DRAFT

In your revision, focus on how well you followed the organization for a summary. Compare your summary with the model summary below. Notice the introduction and the concluding statement and how the writer follows order of importance. Also notice how the writer uses transitions to add information.

> Nicole Chang talks about different kinds of commercial pilots in her article "So You Want to Fly." One kind of commercial pilot is the personal pilot. These pilots are hired by corporations to fly their corporate jets. A corporation's top executives use these jets to fly all over the country and the world for business meetings. Another kind of pilot is employed by public service organizations. Some of these pilots are traffic reporters monitoring the daily commute in many cities. Additionally, they may help law enforcement track down criminals by getting a bird's-eye view of a large area. There are also agricultural pilots. They mostly fly crop dusters. These are planes that spray pesticides on crops to kill insects and diseases that could ruin the crops. Agricultural pilots also spread seeds for reforestation. A more dangerous job is the one that aeromedical pilots have. They fly helicopters as well as airplanes for evacuations, medical and other supply drops, and rescuing people from disaster areas. These are the kinds of pilots discussed in Ms. Chang's article. Becoming a commercial pilot is an interesting career filled with many choices.

Answer the following questions about this summary.

1. Circle the title and author of the article being summarized.

2. Write the four essential points of "So You Want to Fly."

_____
_____
_____
_____

3. Which point discusses the most dangerous job of commercial pilots?

_____

4. Underline the introduction and the concluding statement.

5. Put brackets [ ] around the transitions the writer uses.

Chapter 2: Exposition

Reread your summary paragraph. Follow the directions below to help you revise your first draft.

6. Did you include the title of the article and the author's name in your topic sentence?   Yes   No

7. If not, write a new topic sentence to include the missing information.

   _____

8. Lauren Hauptman uses order of importance to organize her article about the work of EMTs. Did you follow her order when you wrote your draft?   Yes   No

9. If not, what must you do to rewrite your draft to organize it by order of importance?

   _____

   _____

   _____

10. Does your summary include all the essential points from the original article?   Yes   No

11. If not, what do you have to add when you revise your draft?

    _____

    _____

12. Did you include a concluding statement in your summary?   Yes   No

13. If not, write a concluding statement.

    _____

    _____

14. Have you used any transitions that add information?   Yes   No

15. If not, list four transitions that you can add when you write your final draft.

    _____

    _____

Summarizing a Reading Selection

INFORMING

LESSON 4
WRITING YOUR FINAL DRAFT

Before you write your final draft, review what you have learned and practiced in this chapter.

1. What type of writing did you do in this chapter?
   _____

2. What are the two steps you used to organize your summary?
   _____

3. What two organizing tools helped you organize your summary?
   _____

4. Why would a writer use transitions that show where information is being added?
   _____
   _____

5. What do you like about your writing?
   _____
   _____

Before you write your final draft, review the rubric on page 7. It will help you understand what an excellent summary should contain.

WRITE YOUR FINAL DRAFT ON SEPARATE PAPER, OR USE A COMPUTER.

Chapter 2: Exposition

Organizing Pattern:
Spatial Order

CHAPTER 3

Description
Describing a Place

When you write an essay describing a person, place, or thing, you are writing a descriptive essay. This chapter focuses on developing a descriptive essay about a place.

What is the best way to organize a description of a place? Most often, writers use spatial order. In **spatial order,** the things being described are arranged according to their physical positions. Are they to the right or left? Up or down? Near or far? East or west? Note how the writer uses spatial order to describe Antarctica.

> Walking across Antarctica, you would see very little color other than white. However, the ice does not all look the same. There are mountains and cliffs as well as wide plains. Sunlight can make the ice glisten and can create weak shadows. In some places, particularly along the coast, gray rock sticks up out of the ice. If you want to see more color, the best place to look is up, where the sky might be blue. If you are near the coast, of course, you can also look out and see blue water.

The writer uses eight words to show where things are. Cross out *across, along, up, out, up, near,* and *out.* Read the paragraph again. Without these words, you do not get the same idea of what the writer sees.

Notice how the details relate to what a person could see in Antarctica. A good description is filled with details that create a picture of the place, person, or thing you are describing. One kind of detail that will help you in describing places is sensory detail. These are details that appeal to the five senses of sight, sound, smell, taste, and touch. In this chapter, you will be using listing, charts, and mapping to help you organize your description of a place.

DESCRIBING

Try It!

Carefully read the selection "Antarctica: The Ice-Cold South." Write a three-paragraph essay describing a place that is very cold, very hot, very crowded, deserted, very loud, or very quiet. Use sensory details so the reader can clearly picture the place you are describing.

Read It!

Antarctica: The Ice-Cold South

Many people who live in northern climates like to go south for vacations. Often, this is because they want to go to a place that is warm. However, if you go far enough south, you will end up in the coldest place on earth, the South Pole. The South Pole is located in Antarctica, the fifth-largest continent.

Antarctica is almost completely covered by an ice sheet. In most places, the ice is about a mile and a half thick. This ice sheet is called a continental glacier, a large, permanent river of ice. It is really a huge field of ice. Walking across Antarctica, you would see very little color other than white. However, the ice does not all look the same. There are mountains and cliffs as well as wide plains. Sunlight can make the ice glisten and can create weak shadows. In some places, particularly along the coast, gray rock sticks up out of the ice. If you want to see more color, the best place to look is up, where the sky above might be blue. If you are near the coast, of course, you can also look out and see blue water.

If you were in Antarctica in June, July, and August, however, you would have trouble seeing anything. This is wintertime in the southern half of the world. During Antarctica's winter, it is dark almost all day and night. It can still be beautiful, though. Up above are the dazzling Southern Lights, flashes of color that dance through the dark sky.

In summer, on the other hand, there is sunlight all day and night. At night, the sun is down near the horizon, just as it is around sunrise or sunset in the northern hemisphere. Even in summer, however, Antarctica is very cold. In a few places along the coast, though, the water is warm enough for people to swim. This is because of volcanic activity under the water.

However, there are not many people in Antarctica to enjoy this warm water. Antarctica has no permanent human population. More than 15 nations have 40 research centers on the continent. Teams of scientists stay for a year or two in these small buildings and then are replaced by new teams. The best-known inhabitants of Antarctica are penguins. Penguins are flightless birds that live near the coast. They spend much of their time in the water looking for food. But penguins are not at the top of the Antarctic food chain. A penguin looking for food can easily end up becoming someone else's dinner. Swimming around under the water are leopard seals who snap up penguins to eat. Penguins are not completely safe up on the ice, either. Large birds swoop down to grab penguins for dinner.

If you are thinking about going south for a vacation, consider Antarctica. You will see many beautiful and fascinating things there. However, you will not be very warm.

REREAD THE ASSIGNMENT. THINK ABOUT WHAT YOU ARE TO DO.

Step 2. Select Details

The assignment says that your readers should be able to visualize, or picture in their minds, the setting that you write about. To make your writing do this you will need a number of details about that setting. In Step 1, you listed what you see, but it is just a list. Now you need sensory details to make your description come alive. These details should appeal to the senses of sight, sound, touch, smell, and taste. You should also use metaphors and similes to help your readers see the setting.

1. For practice, reread the selection on page 31. Identify four sensory words, two similes, and a metaphor. Write your answers in the chart.

Sensory Words	Similes	Metaphor

Keep these ideas and words in mind as you create your own list of details, similes, and metaphors to use in your descriptive essay.

2. Complete the chart on page 34 by writing in column 1 the things you see in the setting of your movie or book. You listed these items on page 32.

3. In column 2 on page 34, list at least three details for each thing you see. Use sensory words in writing the details. The more work you do in planning, the easier it will be to write your first draft.

Describing a Place

DESCRIBING

What I See	Details That Describe What I See

4. You have identified a number of things that you see and their details. How do you decide which to use? The things and details themselves will help you decide. Which things and details are the most interesting? Which will help the reader to see the setting most clearly?

In column 1, circle three things you want to use to describe the setting.

Step 3. Organize Your Information

1. **Write the spatial order of the three things you have selected to write about. Where are they physically located in the setting you are describing?**

   _____

   _____

   _____

   Now organize the information you listed on page 34 by mapping it.

2. **Write the name of the setting, or place, in the top box.**

3. **Write the three items in their spatial order in the box below. Write the first item in box 1, the second in box 2, and the third in box 3.**

4. **Write the descriptive details from page 34 on the slanted lines.**

5. **Which details can you turn into similes or metaphors? Create the similes or metaphors as you write the details on the map.**

You are now ready to write your first draft.

Describing a Place

LESSON 2
WRITING YOUR FIRST DRAFT

Before you begin to write, review the rubric on page 7. You will evaluate your essay against it.

Guide

Introduction
PARAGRAPH 1
- Identifies the place you are describing
- Includes the name of the book or movie

Body
PARAGRAPH 2
- Presents the sights in spatial order
- Uses details for each thing you see
- Uses sensory words and at least one simile and one metaphor

Conclusion
PARAGRAPH 3
- Wraps up your description

Fluency Tip

Words That Show Place

To help your readers form a mental picture of the setting, use words and phrases that show location.

above
across
along
among
at
behind
below
beside
between
by
down
in front of
in back of
inside
near
outside
over
under
up
to the left
to the right

DESCRIBING

Describing a Place 37

DESCRIBING

LESSON 3
REVISING YOUR DRAFT

Focus on spatial order and sensory details as you revise your essay. Make sure that you have also included at least one simile and one metaphor. Compare your essay with the model essay below. The writer uses spatial order, sensory details, and both a simile and a metaphor (also called literary devices). Read the essay and complete the chart.

A Look at Camp Green Lake

One of my favorite books is Holes by Louis Sachar. The setting is vital to this imaginative story. It takes place at Camp Green Lake, a camp for bad boys. It is really a detention center on barren land, so the boys can dig holes.

"There's no lake at Camp Green Lake" is the first line of the story. About 100 years ago, there was a large lake at this now empty place. It was the largest and bluest lake in Texas. Now it is just old, dried-up wasteland with lots of holes. It looks like a gigantic piece of Swiss cheese. At the entrance to the camp is a small building where the boys must check in. Behind the entrance are a few run-down buildings and some tents. The weather at Camp Green Lake is challenging. During the summer, it is 95 degrees in the shade. There is not much shade at Camp Green Lake. There are only two old oak trees on the eastern edge of the "lake." These trees seem to be standing guard in front of the warden's log cabin. Camp Green Lake is not a place for summer camp.

This is the setting of Holes. The story is a mystery about why the warden wants these holes dug. Is he looking for something? Camp Green Lake is the perfect setting for this adventure.

Question	Model Essay	My Essay
1. Where does the story take place?		
2. List what is being described in spatial order.		
3. List at least five details.		
4. List the words used to show location.		
5. List the simile(s) and metaphor(s).		

LESSON 4

WRITING YOUR FINAL DRAFT

Before you write your final draft, review what you have learned and practiced in this chapter.

1. What type of writing did you do in this chapter?

   _____

2. What organizing pattern did you use in this chapter?

   _____

3. What three tools helped you organize your writing to describe a place?

   _____

4. List four words that can help you describe where something is.

   _____

5. What do you like about your essay?

   _____

   _____

   _____

Before you write your final draft, reread the rubric on page 7. You will evaluate your essay against it. Be sure you know what is needed for an excellent essay.

WRITE YOUR FINAL DRAFT ON SEPARATE PAPER, OR USE A COMPUTER.

CHAPTER 4

Organizing Pattern: Order of Importance

Description
Describing a Person

In this chapter, you will write a descriptive essay about a person. You will choose a person who has an interesting hobby or job. A hobby or job reveals a lot about a person. A hobby can tell us about how talented—artistic, musical, or athletic—someone is. A job can tell us how educated, dedicated, loyal, or interested in people someone is.

To write your description, you will use personality traits. A **personality trait** is a characteristic or quality that makes a person stand out. You can determine personality traits from what you know or observe about a person.

The basic rule of writing a description is to show, not tell. Do not tell the reader a person is fun to be with. Show the reader by giving examples. In the following description, the writer makes a statement about Marcus Irwin. Then she supports it with examples. The examples give us a picture of Irwin's talent.

> Marcus Irwin is a talented guitarist. He plays the bass guitar in the band The Cheeseballs. He can play perfectly the music of the '70s and '80s. Besides disco, he does a wonderful job strumming his guitar and singing folk songs. However, I like it best when he plays classical jazz on his guitar. The air is filled with such interesting, vibrant sounds.

In this lesson you will use **order of importance** to organize your description. You may present the personality traits starting with the most important trait and ending with the least important trait or the other way around.

You will use listing and mapping to help you plan your essay.

Try It!

Read the article "Musical Jordan." Then write a descriptive essay about a person who has an interesting hobby or job. Concentrate on what you know about this person because of her or his job or hobby. The person may be a relative, friend, neighbor, famous person, historical person, or character from a novel, TV program, or movie. Use descriptive details, so the reader understands what you think this job or hobby reveals about the person's personality.

Read It!

Musical Jordan

I have friends who play basketball. I have friends who spend their weekends frantically pounding buttons to win computerized martial arts showdowns. But I do not have any friends that I would rather see on a Saturday afternoon than Jordan. He is an electronic genius, a dedicated musician, and a good business partner. Music is his hobby.

Jordan records music. He does not just burn CDs for friends or play instrumental solos into a tape recorder. Jordan puts together music CDs from scratch. He records each track separately on a program on his computer. Jordan has recorded CDs for several bands at our school. Some people are incapable of hitting the right notes at the right times. This is where Jordan's wizardry comes in. He can synchronize each track, adjusting it so that all the tracks have the same tempo. He can also alter the pitch or volume of a note. This can really come in handy. Some bands are not so good. The lead singer of one of them has a voice like a tree frog. When this happens, Jordan uses all his electronic powers. He can make the singer and the band sound like stars. As I said, Jordan is an electronic genius.

Jordan also plays several instruments. Besides the piano, he plays trumpet and guitar. He practices in the basement, where his father built him his own studio. When he goes down there, Jordan's parents do not see him for hours. He only resurfaces to grab a sandwich. He also records his own music, using drum tracks from his computer. Jordan calls his one-man band Jordan Mania. He is definitely dedicated to his music.

Jordan and I make a great business team. I play guitar and sing songs that I write when I am supposed to be paying attention in class. Jordan and I then record the songs. We listen to music we have previously recorded, find a good part, and put it on our soundtrack. We mix sounds into my songs, too, and then burn a CD. I have convinced my artistic sister to design a cover. We then try to sell the CDs at the local music store. So far, we have had only one buyer. I think it was a relative. We are not discouraged. All businesses have to get started somewhere.

Jordan is my best friend. I respect his electronic know-how, his musical sense, and his willingness to go into business with me. The two of us will someday see our names in neon lights. I am convinced of it.

REREAD THE ASSIGNMENT. THINK ABOUT WHAT YOU ARE TO DO.

LESSON 1
PREWRITING

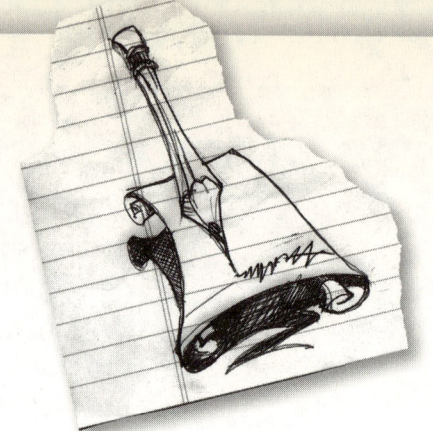

Step 1. Brainstorm

Did you notice that the assignment asks you to write about two things? It asks you to write an essay (1) about a person who has an interesting hobby or job and (2) what that hobby or job reveals about the person. To complete the assignment satisfactorily, you have to do more than just explain what the person does. You have to describe the personality traits that this choice of job or hobby reveals about the person.

For example, Jordan's hobby shows his interest in music. But it shows much more than this. It shows that he is very skilled with electronics, a dedicated musician, and a good business partner. Your essay should describe the person you have chosen in the same way. You must use the person's job or hobby to describe the person's personality.

The assignment suggests some kinds of people to think about as a possible topic:

relative	friend	neighbor
famous person	historical person	character in a novel
TV character	character in a movie	

1. List as many people as you can who have interesting jobs or hobbies. Remember these jobs or hobbies do not have to be unusual. They should (1) be interesting to you and (2) reveal the personality of the person.

Person _____   Hobby/Job _____

_____   _____

_____   _____

_____   _____

_____   _____

_____   _____

Chapter 4: Description

2. Read the list of people and their jobs or hobbies that you wrote on page 42. Which two do you want to write about? Think about how much you know about each person. Which two do you think are the most interesting people and have the most interesting hobbies?

   Select two of the people by placing a checkmark by their names on the list.

3. Write the name of one person and his or her job or hobby on the first line of column 1. Write the other person's name and job or hobby on the first line of column 2.

4. Brainstorm by listing everything that comes to mind when you think of these two people and their jobs or hobbies. These ideas will become the descriptive details you will use in your essay about one of these people.

Describing a Person

DESCRIBING

Step 2. Select Information

Select one of the two people you wrote about on page 43 for your essay. How do you decide? You might choose the person you have observed the most, the one you know the most about, or the one who is easiest to describe in terms of his or her job or hobby. Remember that you are focusing on what the person's hobby or job reveals about him or her.

1. **Whom have you chosen? Write that person's name and hobby or job here.**

   _____

2. What personality traits or qualities would you use to describe this person as revealed by his or her hobby or job? Read the following list of personality traits. If you do not know what some words mean, look them up in a dictionary.

honest	thoughtful	bright	courageous
funny	serious	reliable	bold
humble	friendly	creative	compassionate
confident	successful	patriotic	helpful
energetic	cheerful	loyal	responsible
talented	athletic	hard-working	intelligent

   Circle the traits that best describe the subject of your essay.

3. **If you do not find qualities in the list that fit your subject, add your own ideas.**

   _____ _____ _____

   _____ _____ _____

4. Reread the traits you have circled and any you wrote. Select the three traits you want to use to describe the person you are going to write about. You should choose the three traits that are the most important to you in describing this person.

   Write the three traits here.

   _____

   _____

   _____

Chapter 4: Description

Step 3. Organize Your Essay

You will use order of importance to organize your description. Do you want to organize your essay from the most important to the least important trait, or from the least important to the most important trait? In describing Jordan, the writer develops his ideas from least important to most important.

On page 44, you chose the three most important traits to describe the person in your essay. How can the three most important traits have one that is least important? You cannot write about all three traits at once. You have to decide which one you will write about first, which you will write about second, and which will come third. Organizing your essay from most important to least important or the other way around means deciding on the order in which to put the traits.

Think about the traits. You probably value one more than the other two. Perhaps the person's sense of responsibility is what you respect most. Perhaps it is the person's creativity that is most important to you.

1. Of the three traits you selected on page 44, which is the most important to you?

   Write number 1 next to that trait.

2. Which is less important?

   Write number 2 next to that trait.

3. Which of the three is the least important?

   Write number 3 next to that trait.

4. Now you have to decide the order of importance to use. Do you want to develop your ideas from most important to least important or from least important to most important?
   - Do you want to give your readers the most important information first?
   - Do you want to build up their interest by going from least important to most important?

   Write here the pattern you will use.

   _____

   _____

Mapping the character traits will help you pull all the information together for your description.

5. Write the name of the person and hobby or job you are describing in the top box.

6. Write one personality trait in each box below the main one. Write them in the order of importance you decided on. Put the first trait you want to mention in the box on the left.

7. Reread the list of details you brainstormed on page 43. Write the details you want to use on the slanted lines that extend from each trait box.

8. You should have at least three descriptive details for each personality trait. If you do not, add descriptive details that do not appear on page 43.

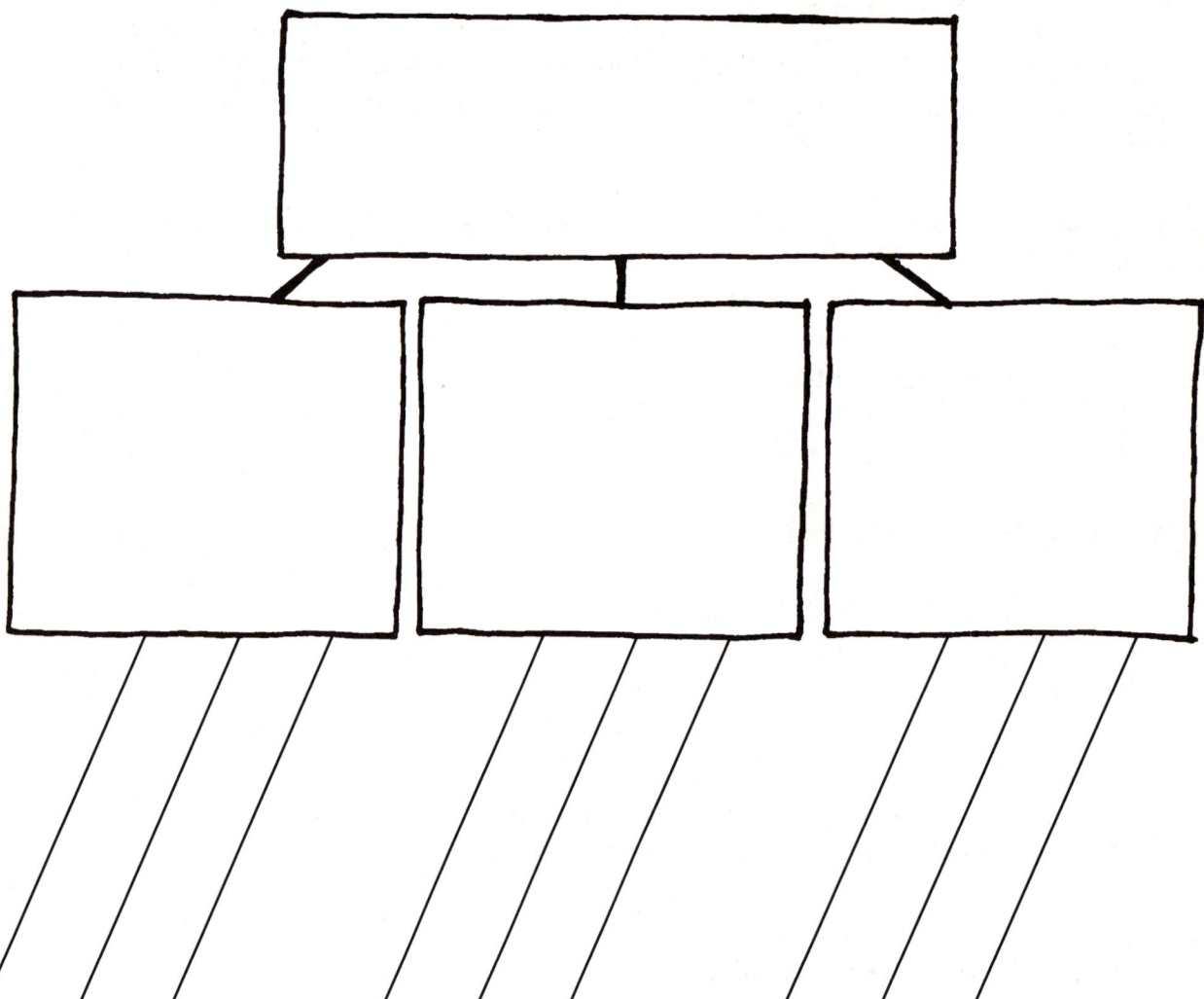

LESSON 2
WRITING YOUR FIRST DRAFT

Before you begin to write, review the rubric on page 7. You will evaluate your essay against it.

Guide

Introduction

PARAGRAPH 1
- States the main idea in a topic sentence
- Identifies the job or hobby
- States the three personality traits

Body

PARAGRAPH 2
- Describes the first trait in detail

PARAGRAPH 3
- Describes the second trait in detail

PARAGRAPH 4
- Describes the third trait in detail

Conclusion

PARAGRAPH 5
- Restates the main idea (the person and what the hobby or job reveals about the person)
- Summarizes the personality traits

DESCRIBING

Fluency Tip

Transitions That Add Information

To help make your descriptive essay read more smoothly, use transitions that add information. These words and phrases will help you connect each new idea to the previous one.

- **additionally**
- **also**
- **another**
- **as well as**
- **besides**
- **for example**
- **for instance**
- **in addition**
- **next**
- **such as**
- **too**

Chapter 4: Description

DESCRIBING

Describing a Person

LESSON 3
REVISING YOUR DRAFT

As you revise your essay, focus on the order of importance. Did you present the three major traits in the order of importance to you? Did you develop your essay by presenting descriptive details to show how the hobby or job reveals the person's personality?

Reread the introductory paragraph from "Musical Jordan."

> I have friends who play basketball. I have friends who spend their weekends frantically pounding buttons to win computerized martial arts showdowns. But I do not have any friends that I would rather see on a Saturday afternoon than Jordan. He is an electronic genius, a dedicated musician, and a good friend and business partner. Music is his hobby.

1. Who is the subject of the essay and what is the hobby or job?

   _____

2. What are the three personality traits that are related to the person's hobby or job?

   _____

   _____

Reread the following paragraph describing one of the personality traits.

> Jordan also plays several instruments. Besides the piano, he plays trumpet and guitar. He practices in the basement, where his father built him his own studio. When he goes down there, Jordan's parents do not see him for hours. He only resurfaces to grab a sandwich. He also records his own music, using drum tracks from his computer. Jordan calls his one-man band Jordan Mania. He is definitely dedicated to his music.

3. What personality trait is described in this paragraph? Be careful. The trait is not mentioned at the beginning of the paragraph.

   _____

4. The writer uses two transition words or phrases in this paragraph. Circle them.

5. In your essay, did you describe what you know about the person because of the person's job or hobby?   Yes   No

6. If not, write a new topic sentence that includes what you know about the person because of the person's job or hobby.

   _____
   _____
   _____

7. Does the rest of your introductory paragraph state the three personality traits that you have selected about the person?   Yes   No

8. If not, rewrite your introductory paragraph. Include your new topic sentence here.

   _____
   _____
   _____
   _____
   _____

9. Does your choice of order of importance (most to least or least to most) develop your ideas clearly?   Yes   No

10. If not, why do you think the organization does not work?

    _____
    _____
    _____

If you decide to change the order, do not just move paragraphs around. Make sure the paragraphs make sense when they are shifted. You may need to rewrite the first or last sentences in a paragraph so the ideas flow from paragraph to paragraph. Using transitions at the beginning of paragraphs will help connect ideas from paragraph to paragraph.

DESCRIBING

LESSON 4
WRITING YOUR FINAL DRAFT

Before you begin to write your final draft, review what you have learned and practiced in this chapter.

1. What type of writing did you do in this chapter?

   _____

2. What pattern did you use to organize your essay?

   _____

3. What three steps did you take to organize your descriptive essay?

   _____

4. What two organizing tools did you use to pull the information together for your essay?

   _____

5. What do you like about what you wrote?

   _____

   _____

   _____

Reread the rubric on page 7. What will make your essay excellent?

WRITE YOUR FINAL DRAFT ON SEPARATE PAPER, OR USE A COMPUTER.

Chapter 4: Description

Organizing Patterns:
**Block Arrangement
Order of Importance**

CHAPTER 5

Exposition
Comparing and Contrasting

When you compare things, people, or events, you are showing how they are the same. When you contrast things, people, or events, you are pointing out their differences. In this chapter, you will compare and contrast snow and rain, looking for their similarities and differences.

People make comparisons and contrasts every day. For example, you compare and contrast when deciding which shirt to wear, which movie to see, which CD to listen to, or which bike to buy. Comparison-and-contrast essays are also common classroom assignments. You might have to compare and contrast two novels in English class or the actions of two monarchs for a history report.

In Chapter 2, you learned that expository writing is writing to inform. **Expository writing** can also be writing to explain. When you write an essay comparing and contrasting things, people, or events, you are writing an expository essay.

There are several ways to organize a comparison-and-contrast essay. In this chapter, you will practice using **block arrangement**. In one paragraph, you compare things. In the next paragraph, you contrast them.

You will use listing, a Venn diagram, and a chart to help you identify information and organize your essay.

Try It!

Read the two articles about snow and rain. Write an essay that compares and contrasts these two weather conditions. Be sure to include details.

Read It!

Snow

How does snow form? Snow requires four conditions to form. First, the atmosphere must have enough molecules of water vapor and dust particles to form ice crystals. A molecule is a tiny particle, or speck. The ice crystals bump into each other and join together. Next, those crystals must fall through layers of air colder than 0° Celsius (32° Fahrenheit). The clouds must be deep. The ice crystals need depth to grow in size as they travel through clouds. Finally, the clouds must have enough moist air to replace what becomes snow. When these four factors are in place, snow forms.

The heaviest snowfall comes from the thickest and darkest clouds. Cumulus clouds are puffy mounds that look like cauliflower. They bring snow showers. Stratus clouds are low, flat, and in layers and carry continuous snow.

As many as 100 individual snow crystals form a single snowflake. No two snowflakes are alike. The size of snowflakes differs and so do their beautiful lacy patterns. However, most snowflakes are six-sided, and all snowflakes are flat.

Rain

How does rain form? About a million tiny water droplets in the air bump together and form raindrops. Rain also forms when snowflakes or other ice particles fall through warm air near the earth.

You can expect rain if the clouds are dark gray. These are cumulonimbus clouds. They are filled with water droplets, ice crystals, and even hail. Cumulonimbus clouds bring thunder, lightning, and heavy rain. A slow, steady rain usually comes from thin, light clouds called nimbostratus clouds.

A raindrop must be at least 0.02 inches (0.5 mm) in diameter. Otherwise, scientists say it is drizzling, not raining. To make one raindrop takes about 700 drizzle drops. If raindrops get too big, they break into smaller drops. The bigger the diameter of the raindrops, the less rain falls. Raindrops begin round but get flatter as they fall.

Scientists who study the weather classify rainfall as light, moderate, or heavy. These labels are based on how much rain falls per hour. Less than 2.5 mm is called a light rain. A moderate rain is between 2.8 and 7.6 mm. Any more than 7.6 mm of rain within an hour is considered a heavy rain. Heavy rains usually do not last more than an hour. Light or moderate rains may last for hours or even days.

REREAD THE ASSIGNMENT. THINK ABOUT WHAT YOU ARE TO DO.

LESSON 1
PREWRITING

Step 1. Identify Differences and Similarities

The assignment asks you to write an essay that explains the differences and similarities between snow and rain. The first article discusses snow, and the second article deals with rain. Neither article compares and contrasts the two weather conditions. You will have to decide for yourself what the differences and similarities are.

To decide, you first need to identify the information in the two articles that you might be able to use. That means listing what each article says about the weather condition it describes. Use the Venn diagram below to help you keep track of the differences and similarities.

1. List the information about snow on the left.

2. List the information about rain on the right.

3. In the center, list information that applies to both snow and rain.

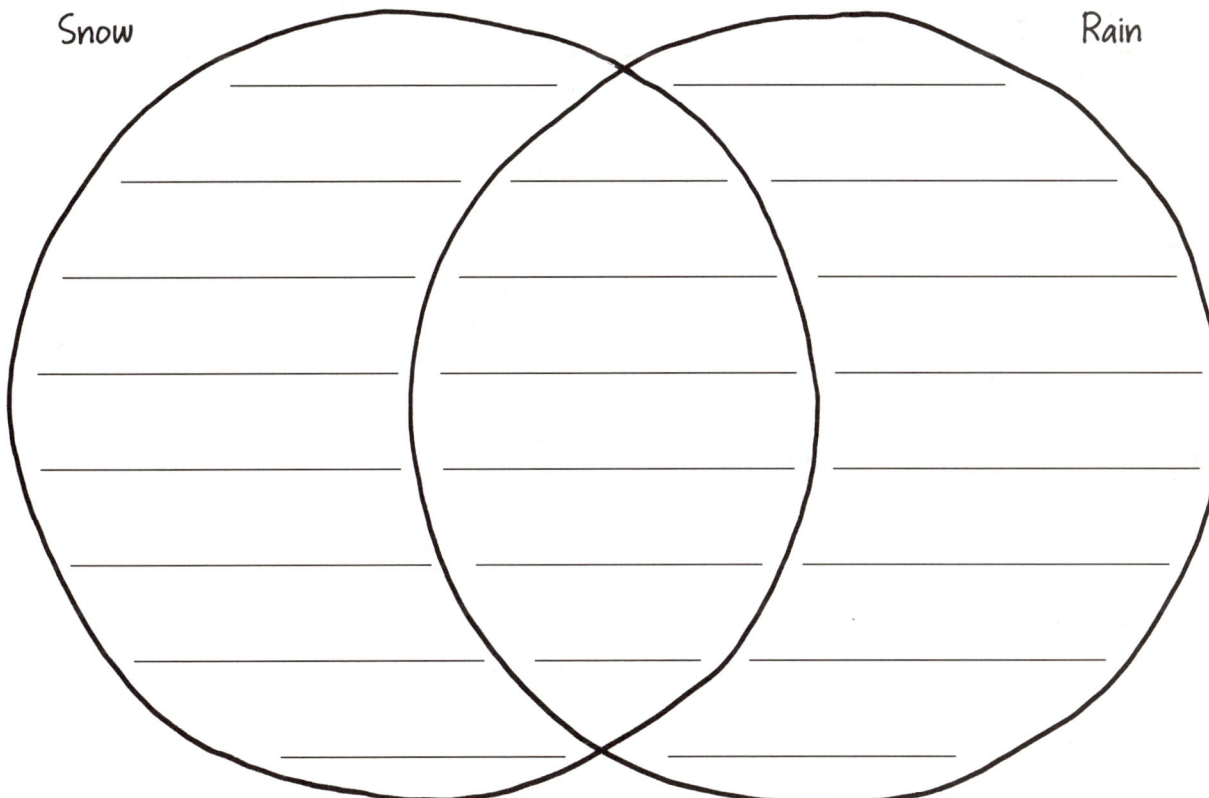

Comparing and Contrasting

Step 2. Select Information

To organize your comparison-and-contrast essay, you are going to use a block arrangement of ideas. One paragraph will explain the similarities. One paragraph will explain the differences.

- For each similarity, you must have a point, or detail, about snow and a point about rain.
- For each difference, you must have a point about snow and a point about rain.

These two paragraphs will make up the body of your essay. You will still need to write an introductory paragraph and a concluding paragraph.

To decide which points to use, review the Venn diagram on page 55. Then follow the directions below.

1. Are there are any points about snow that do not have similar points about rain?

Cross out the points about snow that do not have matching points about rain.

2. Are there are any points about rain that do not have similar points about snow?

Cross out the points about rain that do not have matching points about snow.

The assignment tells you to compare and contrast the two weather conditions. It does not tell you how many points to use. If an assignment does not tell you the number of points you should use, always use at least three points, details, or examples. For this essay you will need

- three points that show how snow and rain are the same
- three points that show how snow and rain are different.

How do you choose which points to use? Review your Venn diagram and evaluate it against your details.

- Which three similarities, or comparisons, seem the most interesting?
- Which three differences, or contrasts, seem the most interesting?

3. Circle the three comparisons that you want to use.

4. Circle the three contrasts that you want to use.

5. You should have three points of comparison and three points of contrast. If you do not, go back to page 55 and work through the steps again.

Step 3. Organize Your Information

Now that you have identified the points you want to use, you have to decide how to organize them. The easiest way is to use the same order that the writer of the article uses. The writer arranges the information in order of importance. She develops her ideas about snow and rain by moving from what is most important to what is least important in her opinion.

1. In the chart below, write the three similarities you are going to use in column 1. List them in order of importance, moving from most important to least important.

2. Column 2 is divided into two blocks. In the left block, write the three differences for snow you plan to use. Write them in the order of importance used by the author of the original article.

3. In the right block, write the three differences for rain you plan to use. Write them in order of importance to match the order in which you wrote the similarities.

Similarities	Differences	
	Snow	Rain

Comparing and Contrasting

EXPLAINING

LESSON 2
WRITING YOUR FIRST DRAFT

Before you begin to write, review the rubric on page 7. You will evaluate your essay against it.

Guide

Introduction

PARAGRAPH 1
- States the focus, or main idea, of the essay in the topic sentence
- Identifies the two items being compared and contrasted

Body

PARAGRAPH 2
- Explains the similarities

PARAGRAPH 3
- Explains the differences

Conclusion

PARAGRAPH 4
- Restates the focus of your essay
- Summarizes the points in the essay

Fluency Tip

Transitions That Show Comparison and Contrast

To help make your comparison-and-contrast essay read more smoothly, use transitions that point out similarities and differences.

SIMILARITIES

as well as
both
in common
in comparison
like
same
similar
too

DIFFERENCES

although
but
even though
however
in contrast
instead
on the other hand
though
unlike
whereas
while
yet

Comparing and Contrasting

LESSON 3
REVISING YOUR DRAFT

What do you think of your essay? As you revise it, focus on the organization of your ideas. To help you, review the following model essay that compares and contrasts kayaks and canoes. As you read, notice how the writer organizes his ideas. Ask yourself if all the comparisons and contrasts include points about both kayaks and canoes.

Kayaks and Canoes

Kayaks and canoes are very similar, but they do have their differences, too. We can easily see the differences and similarities between a sailboat and a speedboat and between a tugboat and a cruise ship. However, the similarities and differences between a kayak and a canoe cannot be seen so easily.

The kayak and canoe have a number of things in common. Both are narrow water vessels. Both are small, human-powered boats. More than one person can paddle a canoe. The same is true for a kayak. The paddlers in both boats face the direction they are traveling.

How are canoes and kayaks different? The canoe is an open boat, whereas the kayak is a covered one. The paddlers of a kayak sit down low in the kayak. In contrast, the paddlers of a canoe sit higher up on a bench-like support in the canoe. Even though paddles are used to propel both vessels, the paddles are different. The paddles used in a canoe have one blade, while the paddles used in a kayak have two blades.

Despite these differences, water enthusiasts all over the world enjoy using kayaks and canoes for both recreation and sport. The word "kayak" comes from an Inuit word meaning "boat of people." But it seems as if both the kayak and the canoe are boats for people.

---

1. **For every point about kayaks, does the writer include a point about canoes?**
   Yes   No

2. **The writer clearly states the focus, or main idea, of the essay. What is the focus of the essay?**

   _____

3. **How many points does the writer use to compare kayaks and canoes?**

   _____

4. **How many points does the writer use to contrast kayaks and canoes?**

   _____

Use an "x" or a ✓ to answer each question for your essay.

Organization and Content Check for Your Essay	Yes	No
5. Have you stated the focus of your essay clearly?		
6. In your comparison paragraph, does every point about snow have a matching point about rain?		
7. In your contrast paragraph, does every point about snow have a difference with rain?		
8. Do you discuss at least three comparisons?		
9. Do you discuss at least three contrasts?		
10. Do you use any transitions to show comparison or contrast?		

11. Look at any rows where you checked "No." What do you need to do to change the "No" to "Yes"?

_____

_____

_____

12. You may have marked all the "Yes" boxes, but are you satisfied with what you wrote? How could you improve your writing?

_____

_____

_____

LESSON 4
WRITING YOUR FINAL DRAFT

Before you begin to write your final draft, review what you have learned and practiced in this chapter.

1. What type of writing did you do in this chapter?

_____

2. What three steps did you take to organize your essay?

_____

3. What three tools did you use to help you organize your writing?

_____

4. Write five transitions that you could use in your writing to show comparison or contrast.

_____

5. What did you like about your writing?

_____

_____

_____

Reread the rubric on page 7. How can you make your essay excellent?

WRITE YOUR FINAL DRAFT ON SEPARATE PAPER, OR USE A COMPUTER.

EXPLAINING

Comparing and Contrasting

CHAPTER 6

Organizing Pattern:
Chronological Order

Exposition
Explaining Cause and Effect

A **cause-and-effect essay** is another type of expository writing. It explains the relationship between two things when one thing makes the other happen. If you complete the sentence "If . . . , then . . .", you are stating a cause-and-effect relationship. For example, "If you do not get enough sleep during the night, then you will be tired the next day."

One cause may result in several effects. For example, the player was unhappy over his contract. As a result, he spoke out against the management of the team in a radio interview. Then he insulted the quarterback in a cable TV interview. He also got into a shouting match in the locker room with a player on his own team. The player's unhappiness led to three actions, or effects.

One cause can also start a chain of cause-and-effect relationships. For example, forgetting to fill up the gas tank results in (1) the car failing to start. Because the car did not start, (2) you are late for school. Because you are late for school, (3) you miss the bus for the field trip. Because you miss the bus for the field trip, (4) you have to sit in study hall all day.

Cause-and-effect essays and reports are favorite assignments of science and social studies teachers. Organizing by chronological order is a useful pattern for cause-and-effect writing.

This chapter gives you more practice with listing and creating a chart as organizing tools.

LESSON 1
PREWRITING

Step 1. Identify Information

The assignment asks you to write an essay about what would happen if you did not study for a test. The cartoon is the prompt for the assignment. It is there to help you think of ideas about the consequences, or effects, of not studying for a test.

Because there is no story and only one idea to the cartoon, you will have to use your imagination, your experience, and your outside knowledge to explain the effects of not studying. You actually do not have a choice. The assignment tells you to do this. Because it does, the amount of information that you bring to the writing of your essay will count when it is graded. If you only write, "I could be grounded for a month," your score will probably not be very high. Taking the time to think about the consequences and plan what you will say will help you write a better essay.

The first step is to identify what is happening in the cartoon.

1. What clues are there that the character should have studied for the test?

_____
_____
_____

2. What did the character do instead?

_____
_____
_____

3. What is the message of the cartoon?

_____
_____
_____

EXPLAINING

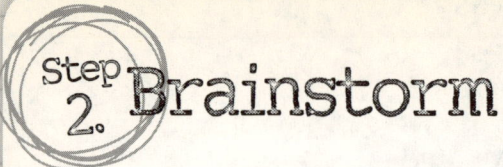
Step 2. Brainstorm

The assignment asks you to imagine the effects of not studying for a test. Remember that a cause can have more than one effect, and it can also set off a chain reaction of causes and effects. Remember also to use your imagination.

Brainstorming is a good way to think of ideas quickly. It allows you to think without worrying if effects are unlikely, unbelievable, or impossible. You want to think of all possible answers to the question:

- What would be the effects if I did not study for a test?

Include as much information as you can and be as specific as possible. Do not just list "will get an F." Be precise. Instead, you can write something like, "an F will get me in big trouble with my parents." Use descriptive words and phrases to paint a picture of the effects for the reader.

1. **Write as many effects as you can that would result from not studying for a test. Remember this act can cause a chain of causes and effects.**

   _____
   _____
   _____
   _____
   _____
   _____
   _____
   _____

2. **Draw a circle around any chains of causes and effects.**

3. Now you have to decide which effects or chain of causes and effects you want to write about in your essay. Think about the answers to the following questions:
   - Which effects or chain is the most interesting?
   - Which effects or chain has the most details?
   - Which would be the easiest to explain?

   Place a ✔ by the three effects (or the chain of causes and effects) that you want to use.

Chapter 6: Exposition

Step 3. Organize Your Ideas

Once you have selected the ideas you are going to use in your essay, you must decide how to develop them. Chronological order is the usual way to present a cause and its effects. Because a cause makes something happen, it comes before the effect or effects.

1. **Write the cause on the line above the following chart.**

2. **Write your three effects or chain of effects across the top part of the chart. List them in the order in which they will occur if you do not study for a test.**

Cause: _____

The Consequences (Effects) of This Cause:

An essay without details is boring. You need to add interest to your essay by adding descriptive details.

3. **List details for each effect in the bottom part of your chart. Write at least three details for each effect.**

Explaining Cause and Effect

EXPLAINING

LESSON 2
WRITING YOUR FIRST DRAFT

Before you begin to write, review the rubric on page 7. You will evaluate your essay against it.

Guide

Introduction

PARAGRAPH 1
- States the cause in the topic sentence
- States the three main effects in time order

Body

PARAGRAPH 2
- States the first effect
- Includes details that describe the effect

PARAGRAPH 3
- States the second effect
- Includes details that describe the effect

PARAGRAPH 4
- States the third effect
- Includes details that describe the effect

Conclusion

PARAGRAPH 5
- Restates the cause
- Sums up the effects and how you feel

Fluency Tip

Transitions That Show Cause and Effect

To make your essay read more smoothly, use transitions that show cause and effect. Use some of these to signal cause-and-effect relationships:

as a consequence

as a result

because

because of

consequently

on account of

so

then

therefore

Explaining Cause and Effect

LESSON 3
REVISING YOUR DRAFT

The revision process is an important stage in writing your essay. It is the time to (1) improve the organization, (2) rewrite sentences to make your ideas clearer, (3) include more details to make the essay more interesting, and (4) add transitions to make your ideas flow more smoothly. Compare your essay with the model essay below about the effects of having a bad attitude. Analyze how the writer organizes and describes the effects of her attitude. Notice how she uses details and transitions.

Bad Attitude

Ever since I was a little kid, I have wanted to play basketball. Because I am such a good all-around athlete, I thought that was all I needed. As a result, I did not apply much effort, and I lost out because of it.

I believed that I was so good that I did not need to practice or train on my own. Once I made the team, I stopped shooting baskets in the park. As a result, my shooting was off. I had the lowest free-throw percentage on the team. I also stopped running and lifting weights. Because of this, my stamina and strength suffered. A few trips up and down the floor left me gasping for air.

One of the worst effects of my attitude was that I thought I could skip team practices. This made the other players angry and annoyed the coach. I was told that my attitude was harmful to the team. I was not a team player. Consequently, I was not a good representative for the school.

Finally, I lost my place on the starting team for the second half of the season. The coach felt I did not deserve to be a starter. I did not have the commitment to the team. Team members did not respect me because of my attitude. My attitude resulted in my becoming a bench warmer rather than a starter.

My poor attitude resulted in not practicing, not training, and not attending all the team practices. The worst consequence was losing my place as a starter and becoming a bench warmer. I have learned my lesson and I have changed my attitude. Next year, I will practice, practice, practice—on my own and with the team.

1. What does the writer have a bad attitude about?

_____

2. What are the effects, or consequences, of the writer's bad attitude?

_____

_____

3. List two details that the writer uses to describe the first effect.

_____

_____

EXPLAINING

4. How many details does the writer use to describe the second effect?

   _____

5. Explain one thing that you think that this writer did well in her essay.

   _____

   _____

Now analyze your own essay. Complete the following checklist by placing an "x" or a ✔ in the correct column.

Organization and Content Check for Your Essay	Yes	No
6. Have you stated the focus of your essay clearly?		
7. Will your introduction get the attention of readers?		
8. Did you include at least three effects?		
9. Did you include at least two details for each effect?		
10. Does your conclusion sum up the effects?		
11. Did you include how you feel about the consequences?		
12. Did you use any cause-and-effect transitions?		

13. If you have any "No's," what can you do to change them to "Yes's"?

    _____

    _____

14. You may have marked all the "Yes" boxes, but are you satisfied with what you wrote? Think about the details in your essay. What could you add or change to improve your essay?

    _____

    _____

Chapter 6: Exposition

LESSON 4
WRITING YOUR FINAL DRAFT

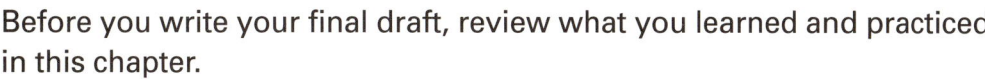

Before you write your final draft, review what you learned and practiced in this chapter.

1. What type of writing did you do in this chapter?
   _____

2. What three steps helped you organize your cause-and-effect essay?
   _____

3. What two organizing tools helped you pull together your ideas for your cause-and-effect essay?
   _____

4. List five transitions that you can use to show cause and effect.
   _____

5. What do you like about what you have written?
   _____
   _____
   _____

Before you write your final draft, review the rubric on page 7. What do you need to do to take your essay to the next level?

WRITE YOUR FINAL DRAFT ON SEPARATE PAPER, OR USE A COMPUTER.

Explaining Cause and Effect

CHAPTER 7

**Organizing Pattern:
Problem-to-Solution Order**

Persuasion

Identifying a Problem and Offering a Solution

A **problem-solution essay** has two and sometimes three parts to it. First, a problem-solution essay informs the reader of an existing problem. Then it proposes one or more solutions to the problem. If the writer wants the reader to adopt the solution, the essay includes a **call to action.**

A problem-solution essay that is persuasive

- explains the problem
- proposes one or more solutions
- encourages the reader to support a particular solution.

Planning and writing a problem-solution essay require more than just organizing your ideas. You, the writer, must

- understand the problem
- think critically about it in order to develop one or more solutions
- be creative in developing that solution or solutions.

The best way to organize a problem-solution essay is to present the problem and then offer the solution. If you want the reader to do something, you close with a call to action.

Speeches are often arranged in this way. A candidate for office identifies the problems with the person who is already in office. The candidate then offers himself or herself as the solution and asks voters to elect him or her.

In this chapter, you will use listing and a chart as your organizing tools.

Try It!

Read the following selection "Global Warming." Then write a problem-solution essay about global warming. Take the position that something must be done to reduce greenhouse gases. Offer a solution that your community can do and give reasons to support your solution. Then ask your community to act on your solution. Use information from the article and your own experience.

Read It!

Global Warming

Global warming refers to the increase in the temperature of the Earth brought about by natural and human activities. Scientists believe that human activities contribute greatly to the warming of the Earth.

To understand global warming, it is necessary to know how the Earth and the Sun interact. The Sun heats the Earth. The Earth absorbs most of this heat and reflects the rest back into space. However, greenhouse gases trap some of the reflected heat in the Earth's atmosphere. Greenhouse gases are vital for life on this planet. Without them, the temperature would be much lower, and the Earth would not be able to support life as we know it. However, in the past century the Earth has experienced a tremendous increase in greenhouse gases, such as carbon dioxide and nitrous oxide. Human activity such as burning fuel for energy creates these gases. The United States produces more greenhouse gases per person than any other nation. This increase in greenhouse gases, especially carbon dioxide, is causing global warming.

Scientists warn of many problems that could result from global warming. The effects will vary widely by region. Some parts of the world may suffer from drought and crop failures. Other places may experience more frequent and intense rainstorms and hurricanes. Areas along the world's coasts may flood because of rising sea levels. In fact, the sea level is likely to rise two feet along most of the U.S. coast in the next century.

Scientists believe that human activities contribute greatly to global warming. The Environmental Protection Agency (EPA) states that for each person in the United States, 6.6 tons of greenhouse gases are emitted every year. However, individuals can change their behaviors. The following are some things people can do:

- Buy energy-saving refrigerators, washing machines, and faucets.
- Use fluorescent lights instead of regular light bulbs.
- Recycle cans, bottles, plastic, cardboard, and paper.
- Buy food with the least amount of packaging.
- Walk or use a bike instead of driving.
- Do several errands at once to avoid multiple car trips.
- Turn off lights when leaving a room.
- Lower the house temperature in winter and raise it in summer to use less energy for heat and air conditioning.
- Buy recycled products such as paper goods.
- Reuse items such as bottles and plastic or paper bags.

REREAD THE ASSIGNMENT. THINK ABOUT WHAT YOU ARE TO DO.

Identifying a Problem and Offering a Solution

PERSUADING

LESSON 1
PREWRITING

Step 1. Identify the Problem

1. What is the reason for writing a problem-solution essay?

_____
_____
_____
_____
_____

2. What is the problem the article discusses?

_____

3. Why is this a problem?

_____
_____
_____
_____
_____
_____

4. What is causing the problem?

_____
_____

Step 2. Brainstorm

The assignment tells you to "offer a solution that your community can do." A solution means that you have to think of a project that people in your community could carry out by working together. The article gives you 10 suggestions about what people can do to reduce global warming. You could use one of them as the basis of the project for your essay. An assignment will not always give you information like this, but take of advantage of it when it does.

1. Write the 10 suggestions from page 75 in column 1 below.

2. Now brainstorm how you can turn these suggestions into a project that your community could do. In column 2 write some ideas about how each suggestion could be turned into a project.

Ways to Reduce Global Warming	Ways to Turn Suggestions into Projects
1.	
2.	
3.	
4.	
5.	
6.	
7.	
8.	
9.	
10.	

The assignment says that you are to offer one solution. The list above will help you decide which suggestion is the best to develop into a project. Reread your chart and think about the answers to the questions on page 78.

Identifying a Problem and Offering a Solution

- Which ideas are the most interesting to you?
- Which ideas would be the easiest for you to develop into a project?
- Are there any ideas that you do not think would work as a project?
- Which ideas seem more suitable for a group of people rather than for one person?
- Which ideas involve several details that will help you write a good essay?

The safest thing to do at this stage in your prewriting is to choose three ideas. That way, you will not waste a lot of time trying to make one idea work. If you cannot think of enough details to use in a well-developed essay for one idea, you will not have to start all over. You can use one of the other ideas instead.

3. Choose three project ideas from your list on page 77. Circle them.

4. Write the three ideas in column 1. Brainstorm ways that each idea could be turned into a community project. Write the details in column 2. Use another sheet of paper if you have more than three. The assignment says to use your own experience. Figuring out the details of your project is a good way to satisfy this part of the assignment.

Possible Projects	Details for Each Project
1.	
2.	
3.	

Step 3. Organize Your Information

PERSUADING

You have identified three projects and details to support each one. Which project do you think will work the best? Use the following questions to help you decide:
- Which solution seems to be the easiest for the community to do?
- Which solution seems to be the most practical for the community to do?

1. **On the chart on page 78, circle the project you want to include in your essay.**

2. On page 76 you identified the problem that this project is meant to help reduce. The problem should be stated in the topic sentence in your introductory paragraph.

   Write your topic sentence, including the problem.

   _____

   _____

3. Review the details you wrote on page 78 to describe your project, which is your solution. You need to put the details in the order you want to develop them in your essay. For this type of essay, you could use either order of importance or chronological order.

   How will you organize your details? _____

4. **Go back to page 78. Number the details for the project you selected in the order you want to use them.**

5. Your concluding paragraph will restate the problem and your project, which is your solution. The conclusion should also include a call to action. Write your call-to-action sentence.

   _____

   _____

6. Have you satisfied all the parts of the assignment? Reread the assignment. Then reread this page for the information you are going to include.

   Have you included everything called for in the assignment?   Yes   No

7. **If not, what do you still need to do?**

   _____

Identifying a Problem and Offering a Solution

PERSUADING

LESSON 2
WRITING YOUR FIRST DRAFT

Before you begin to write, review the rubric on page 7. You will evaluate your essay against it.

Guide

Introduction

PARAGRAPH 1
- Identifies the problem
- States the solution/project you are proposing

Body

PARAGRAPH 2
- Explains the solution/project and how it will work in detail

Conclusion

PARAGRAPH 3
- Restates the problem
- Restates the solution by introducing it with a statement such as, "There is no doubt this solution will . . ."
- Includes a call to action

Fluency Tip

Problem-Solution Signal Words and Phrases

To help make your problem-solution essay read more smoothly, use words and phrases that signal problems and solutions.

another issue

a/the/one problem

another problem

another possibility

a/the/one solution

another solution

in addition

consequently

for this reason

for these reasons

for example

for instance

PERSUADING

Identifying a Problem and Offering a Solution

PERSUADING

LESSON 3
REVISING YOUR DRAFT

What do you think of your essay? In revising your essay, focus on how clearly you present the problem and your solution/project. Be sure that you explain your solution fully and include reasons the public should act on your solution. Compare your draft with the model essay below to see how the writer has developed her solution about paying for crossing guards.

Crossing Guards

The city council and the school board face a big problem. City schools are going to lose their crossing guards. In the past, the city council has paid for school crossing guards. However, the council no longer has enough money to do this. Neither does the school board. Both groups understand the importance of the guards. However, they do not know where the money will come from. The school board says that it can come up with half the money. Where will the rest of the money come from? One solution is the business community.

The schools in this city are excellent. Consequently, many people want to live in this community. Real estate agents use the schools as a reason to buy homes here. Why not ask the real estate companies to donate money to the crossing-guard program? In addition, other businesses in the community could donate money according to their size. For instance, the two large grocery stores and three large drug stores in our city could contribute more than the small hardware store or the bakery. Finally, restaurants could contribute part of the money they make in one day.

City schools will lose their crossing guards because the city and the school board do not have the money to pay for them. Combining money from the school board and local businesses is a great solution to the crossing-guard problem. The safety of children walking to and from school should be a major concern for everybody. Sharing the solution will not cause a hardship for any one group. It will also allow our city to keep a program that is really needed. The time is now for businesses to help pay for the school crossing-guard program. If they do this, they can help make sure that our schoolchildren are safe.

Answer the following questions about this essay.

1. Where is the problem first stated?

_____

2. What is the problem?

_____

3. What solution does the writer suggest?

_____

4. Write two of the details used to support the solution (reasons the solution is a good one).

   _____

   _____

5. Put brackets [ ] around the sentence that restates the solution in the conclusion.

6. Underline the sentence that contains the call to action.

7. Circle the five words or phrases that the writer uses to signal a problem or solution.

Complete the following chart about your own essay. Use an "x" or a ✔ to answer each question for your essay.

Organization and Content Check for Your Essay	Yes	No
8. Do you state the problem clearly?		
9. Do you state your solution clearly?		
10. Do you include at least three details to support your solution/project?		
11. Do you include a clearly stated call to action?		
12. Do you use any words and phrases that signal the problem or solution?		

13. Look at any rows where you checked "No." What do you need to do to change the "No" to "Yes"?

    _____

    _____

14. You may have marked all the "Yes" boxes, but are you satisfied with what you wrote? How could you improve your writing?

    _____

    _____

Identifying a Problem and Offering a Solution

LESSON 4
WRITING YOUR FINAL DRAFT

Before you begin to write your final draft, review what you have learned and practiced in this chapter.

1. What type of writing did you do in this chapter?
   _____
   _____

2. What three steps did you take to organize your problem-solution essay?
   _____
   _____
   _____

3. What two tools did you use to help you organize your ideas?
   _____
   _____

4. List four problem-solution words and phrases that you could use to signal the important points in a problem-solution essay.
   _____
   _____
   _____

5. What do you like about your writing?
   _____
   _____

Review the rubric on page 7. What parts of your essay are you finding difficult to complete successfully? Concentrate on them in your revision.

WRITE YOUR FINAL DRAFT ON SEPARATE PAPER, OR USE A COMPUTER.

Chapter 7: Persuasion

Organizing Pattern:
Logical Order

CHAPTER 8

Persuasion

Writing a Letter to Persuade

The purpose of **persuasive writing** is to convince someone to believe something or to do something. You want your reader to adopt your point of view. Good persuasive writing
- includes logical reasoning and evidence to support your point of view
- recognizes and answers possible objections to your point of view
- calls for the reader to adopt your point of view and do something
- includes enough information so the reader knows exactly what he or she is supposed to do.

Editorials, letters to the editor, letters of complaint to businesses, political speeches, and political Web sites use persuasive writing. Advertisements also use persuasive writing.

How is persuasive writing organized? One pattern of organization is **logical order**. Each idea and paragraph flows reasonably into the next. The development of ideas makes sense as the reader reads through the essay. No idea is out of place, for example:

> Students who play on a school team are excused from physical education classes. Marilyn is on the softball team. Therefore, Marilyn is excused from physical education class.

The third statement makes sense because of the first two statements. This is an example of **logical order**.

Listing and a chart will help you put your ideas in logical order.

PERSUADING

Try It!

Your state legislature is considering a bill to ban cell phone use while driving. Read the article "Juggling the Phone and the Wheel." Then write a persuasive letter to your state senator asking her to support this bill. Use information from the article and your own knowledge to write the letter.

Address your letter to The Honorable Marissa Young, State Senate Office Building, 4305 Cactus Avenue, Phoenix, AZ 85008

Read It!

Juggling the Phone and the Wheel

Have you ever had this experience? A driver cuts you off in traffic. He is holding a cell phone in one hand and the steering wheel in the other. He is also laughing over something he has heard on his phone. Or how about this? You are crossing the street, and are forced to jump out of the way of a car screeching to a halt inches from your knees. You look up and the driver is dialing her phone. Operating a car and a cell phone at the same time is as hazardous as it looks.

In order to dial a phone number, a driver must take his or her eyes off the road. In addition, the driver may become distracted by the conversation. A study suggests that drivers who use cell phones are four times more likely to have accidents than drivers who do not use cell phones while driving. The risk is not reduced when drivers use hands-free phones. In fact, a study showed that drivers using hands-free phones had to redial calls 40 percent of the time. This is more than twice as often as drivers with hand-held phones. Other studies have discovered even more troubling data. Drivers who talked on hands-free phones were 18 percent slower in braking than drivers who were not using a phone. Drivers with hands-free cell phones were also less likely to remember seeing people on the street, billboards, and other roadside landmarks.

More and more people are using cell phones while driving, thus increasing the chances of cell phone–related collisions. Cell phone users jumped from 4.3 million in 1990 to more than 200 million by 2005. Because of this increase, many states have proposed banning the use of cell phones in motor vehicles. By 2005, for example, more than two thirds of the states had reviewed bills that would restrict cell-phone use while driving. Colorado, Delaware, Maryland, and Tennessee outlawed their use by young drivers. Other states are also considering such legislation. The state of New York has completely banned the use of hand-held cell phones while driving. Drivers caught disobeying the law are fined.

Some people claim that using cell phones in a car is no less hazardous than eating or talking to passengers. Several studies show, however, that this is not the case. These studies have found that using cell phones and other wireless devices is more likely to cause a car accident than other distractions. As the use of wireless devices grows, this will become an increasingly important issue.

REREAD THE ASSIGNMENT. THINK ABOUT WHAT YOU ARE TO DO.

LESSON 1
PREWRITING

Step 1. Identify Information

Audience and purpose are two important factors that every writer should keep in mind before setting pen to paper or fingers to keyboard. As a writer, you should be aware of your **audience,** the person or persons who will be reading your writing. This is especially true when you are creating a persuasive piece of writing. You must know who your audience is so that you can shape your arguments to appeal to that audience. A state senator will have different concerns about cell phone use in cars than the president of a cell-phone company.

1. Identify your audience for this assignment. To whom are you writing this letter?

_____

2. Identify your purpose in writing this letter. What is that purpose?

_____

In writing a persuasive piece, you may also have to identify reasons someone might oppose what you want. You will have to answer these objections in your writing.

3. Reread the last paragraph of the article. Identify what supporters of cell phones say about using cell phones while driving. Write that information here.

_____

_____

_____

4. List your own reason or reasons for supporting the bill. This information will become the basis for the second paragraph of your letter.

_____

_____

_____

Writing a Letter to Persuade

PERSUADING

Step 2. Brainstorm

A good piece of persuasive writing lays out evidence to support your point of view. It also answers the objections of opponents. The article on page 86 lists only one objection to banning cell phone use while driving. What other objections can you think of? There are two reasons to add more objections. First, your letter will be stronger if you include more objections that opponents might use. Second, the assignment says to use your own knowledge. Adding possible objections and explaining why they are wrong is one to way to satisfy that part of the assignment.

1. In column 1 below, rewrite the information from number 3 on page 87.

2. Brainstorm other reasons people use cell phones while driving. List those reasons in column 1 as other objections to banning cell phone use in cars.

3. Now brainstorm reasons that you could use to answer objections to banning cell phones. People might claim that (1) cell phones are not dangerous, or (2) they need to use cell phones while driving. How will you answer those objections? Write those reasons in column 2.

4. In addition, your letter must explain why the senator should act and support legislation to ban cell phones while driving. Brainstorm the reasons (benefits) for making it illegal to use a cell phone while driving. Write those ideas in column 3.

Objections to the Ban	Answers	Benefits

Chapter 8: Persuasion

Step 3. Organize Your Essay

You will be using logical order to organize your essay. Logical order means one idea leads to another in a way that makes sense. Sentences are presented in an order that makes it easy to connect the ideas.

Use the following chart to organize your ideas for your letter. You may find that you do not need to use all the ideas you brainstormed on page 88. Also add your ideas from page 87 about why you are asking the senator to support the bill. Write your ideas in logical order, the way you think they will make the most sense in your letter.

Your Reasons for Asking for the Senator's Support	Answers to Objections	Reasons (Benefits) to Support the Bill

LESSON 2
WRITING YOUR FIRST DRAFT

Before you begin to write, review the rubric on page 7. You will evaluate your essay against it.

_____
[your street address]
_____
[city, state, zip code]

_____
[date]

_____
[name of addressee]
_____
[organization]
_____
[street address]
_____
[city, state, zip code]
_____:
[salutation]

_____
_____
_____
_____
_____
_____
_____
_____
_____

Guide

For heading, salutation, and closing, see pages 90 and 92.

Introduction

PARAGRAPH 1
- States your opinion and the purpose of your letter in the topic sentence

Body

PARAGRAPH 2
- Gives reasons for your opinion

PARAGRAPH 3
- Answers objections to your opinion

PARAGRAPH 4
- Gives reasons (benefits) the senator should support your request

Conclusion

PARAGRAPH 5
- Asks the senator directly to take action
- Restates the benefits of this action

Writing a Letter to Persuade

PERSUADING

Fluency Tip

Signal Words and Phrases That Emphasize a Point

To help call attention to important points in your persuasive letter, use some of the following signal words and phrases. They will make your writing move smoothly and logically from one idea to the next.

again

for this reason

in addition

in fact

in summary

to emphasize

to repeat

truly

_____
[closing]

_____
[signature]

Chapter 8: Persuasion

LESSON 3
REVISING YOUR DRAFT

In thinking about how to revise your persuasive letter, focus on four things. Do you present your opinion clearly? Do you answer objections clearly and completely? Do you state the action you want the senator to take? Are your ideas presented in logical order? Read the model letter below and use it to rate the quality of your letter.

BENJAMIN FRANKLIN SCHOOL
11103 INDEPENDENCE DRIVE
PHILADELPHIA, PA 19104

November 30, 2006

Ms. Paula Solano
321 Fourth Street
Philadelphia, PA 19101

Dear Ms. Solano:

    Your dedication and hard work are the main reasons that the Benjamin Franklin Parent-Teacher Organization has been so successful. For this reason, the nominating committee of the PTO of Benjamin Franklin School would like to nominate you for president. We hope you will agree.

    The committee believes that you possess the qualities of a strong leader. You are organized, dependable, and diplomatic. In addition, you are a good public speaker. You have served on the PTO board for three years, so you have the experience and knowledge of how the organization operates. In summary, we need your leadership, experience, and dedication.

    We realize that you are a busy woman. You are involved in two community groups and do volunteer work at the hospital. You are on the PTO board already, and this would only mean a change of duties. We also realize you have three active children who take up your time. However, the work with the PTO will directly benefit them.

    We know you are the person to continue the excellent record of our PTO. You will continue the clear and open communication we have with the principal, the teachers, and the parents. We know you will maintain our good relationship with the city council and the Department of Recreation. We are also sure you will continue the successful fund-raising programs that support our school.

    We would like you to be the leader of our PTO. Please call me at 555-5245 with your decision, so I can place your name on the ballot.

Sincerely,

Teresa Khalifa

Chair, PTO Nominating Committee

The writer of the model letter follows the organization of a good persuasive letter. She
1. states clearly in the introduction her purpose for writing the letter
2. lists some reasons that Ms. Solano might not agree to be nominated for president
3. offers arguments to remove each possible objection
4. lists the benefits if Ms. Solano were to be nominated and then elected
5. concludes with a direct appeal to Ms. Solano to run.

How does your letter compare to the model letter? Complete the following chart to find out. The chart will help you identify areas for improvement in you letter.

Organization and Content Check for Your Essay	Yes	No
1. Does the introduction state the purpose of your letter?		
2. Does the letter list at least some of the objections that people who support driving with cell phones might raise?		
3. Does the letter answer each objection?		
4. Does the letter state the benefits of the action you want taken?		
5. Would your letter be more convincing if you stated more benefits?		
6. Does the letter conclude with an appeal to support the bill?		

7. If you answered "No" to any of the questions, explain how you can improve that part of you letter.

_____
_____
_____
_____

LESSON 4
WRITING YOUR FINAL DRAFT

Before you begin to write your final draft, review what you have learned and practiced in this chapter.

1. What type of writing did you do in this chapter?

_____

2. What three steps did you use to organize your persuasive letter?

_____

3. What two tools did you use to help you organize your letter?

_____

4. What are five words or phrases that you can use to emphasize points in persuasive writing?

_____

_____

5. What do you like about your letter?

_____

_____

_____

Review the rubric on page 7. What do you need to do to improve your draft so it will rate a top score?

WRITE YOUR FINAL DRAFT ON SEPARATE PAPER, OR USE A COMPUTER.

Writing a Letter to Persuade

APPENDIX

Transitions

Transitions are words and phrases that connect one idea to the next. They are like bridges. They help your ideas flow smoothly from sentence to sentence and paragraph to paragraph. Get in the habit of using them as you write and you will find that your writing is easier to understand and reads more smoothly.

Transitions That Show Time Order
- a few days ago
- a week ago
- after
- after a while
- at last
- a while ago
- before
- during
- finally
- first, second, third, . . .
- immediately
- later
- next
- right away
- soon, sooner
- then, by then
- today, yesterday, tomorrow

Transitions That Add Information
- additionally
- along with
- also
- another
- as well as
- besides
- finally
- first, second, third, . . .
- for example
- for instance
- however
- in addition
- in fact
- last
- more/most importantly
- next
- too

Transitions That Show Cause and Effect
- as a consequence
- as a result
- because
- because of
- consequently
- on account of
- so
- then
- therefore

Transitions That Show Comparison and Contrast

Similarities
- as well as
- both
- in common
- in comparison
- like
- same
- similar
- too

Differences
- although
- but
- even though
- however
- in contrast
- instead
- on the other hand
- though
- unlike
- while
- yet

Signal Words and Phrases

Problem-Solution Signal Words and Phrases
To help make your problem-solution essay read more smoothly, use words and phrases that signal problems and solutions.

a/the/one problem
another problem
another issue

a/the/one solution
another solution
another possibility

in addition

consequently
for this reason
for these reasons

for instance
for example

Signal Words and Phrases That Emphasize a Point
To help make your persuasive letter signal important points, use some of the following words and phrases. They will make your writing move smoothly and logically from one idea to the next.

again
for this reason
in addition
in fact
in summary
to emphasize
to repeat
truly